Sugar Inspira

D0533765

Sugar Embroidery

ADRIAN WESTROPE & PAT TRUNKFIELD

MEREHURST

Dedication

I would like to thank my Mum, Dad, Neil and Donna, and all who have helped to keep me together over the last year. I also wish to thank Pat for her help, laughter and friendship. This book is for sugarcrafters world wide. Adrian

To Clive and Ian for their patience, support, encouragement and understanding. Special thanks to Adrian for inviting me to share this opportunity. Pat

First published 1996 by Merehurst Limited
Ferry House, 51–57 Lacy Road, Putney,
London SW15 1PR

Copyright © Merehurst Limited 1996
ISBN 1-85391-574-2

A catalogue record for this book is available from the British Library.

Editor: Helen Southall
Design: Anita Ruddell
Photography by James Duncan

Colour separation by Bright Arts, Hong Kong
Printed in Hong Kong by Wing King Tong

Contents

INTRODUCTION 4
Techniques 4
Equipment 5
Design Ideas 5
Basic Recipes 6

Introduction

Copied in sugar, the intricate stitches and techniques of needlecraft can be used to stunning effect on celebration cakes and sugar ornaments of all kinds.

For sugar embroidery, the threads and silks of needlework are replaced by finely piped royal icing. Many different stitches and other needlecraft techniques can be reproduced in icing, from delicate lace, satin stitch and smocking, to bold colour beadwork and cross stitch.

Advanced piping skills are not essential for the designs in this book. With a little practice, brush embroidery, linework and finely piped dots and crosses become easy. All you need is a steady hand and plenty of patience; the results will always be worthwhile.

Techniques

Choosing a design

Choose simple, uncomplicated designs at first, limiting the embroidery to a small area, such as on a plaque, card or badge. The designs you use can be based on your own ideas or illustrations, or you can copy pictures or diagrams from books, magazines, greetings cards or wrapping paper.

Transferring a design

Unless you are very experienced at piping freehand, you will need to mark the outline of your chosen design on the cake, plaque or other surface before you start piping. For brush embroidery on the top or side of a cake, the simplest way to do this is to use flower and leaf cutters to indent the surface of the sugarpaste (rolled fondant) while it is still soft. For counted beadwork or dot embroidery, where the whole area of the design will be covered with icing, the design can first be marked out with coloured food pens. Marking out designs first avoids continuously having to count squares, which can be very tiring on the eyes.

Another method of transferring an illustration from the page of a book or magazine is to trace it on to tracing paper, and then, holding the pattern in position, use a scriber or other sharp implement to mark the design through the paper on to the icing beneath. The very light lines made by the scriber act as a guide and are easily piped over.

Cross stitch designs are much easier to copy if they are first redrawn on to graph paper, replacing the symbols with colours. When piping the designs, you do not always need to find the centre of the picture you are copying; you only need to work out the maximum height and width. Find the same by counting the piped or indented squares on the marked cake surface, and pipe the design from top to bottom.

Copying fabrics

Some fabrics are best copied using a combination of piping and cut pieces of mexican paste applied directly to the cake's surface (see the Belgian-Style Lace Cake on page 22). Small off-set pieces can be added to the design once the basic

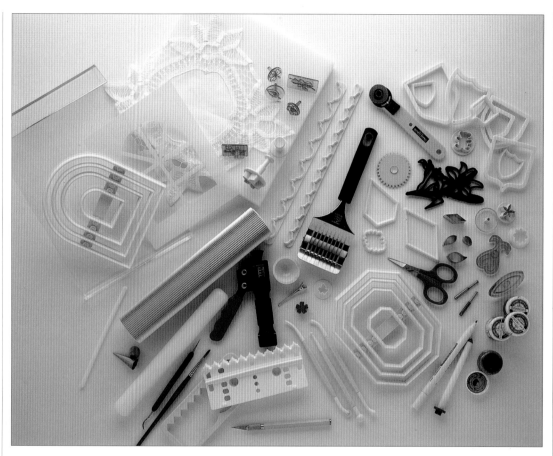

pattern has dried. The icing must not be too soft or the definition of the design will be lost.

Using colour

Royal icing, mexican paste, flower paste and sugarpaste (rolled fondant) can be coloured as required with paste food colours. Do not hesitate to use bold, bright colours and to experiment by blending different colours together. Adding a hint of cream or brown to white icing can give a design an 'antique lace' look, where appropriate.

Equipment

The most important items required for sugar embroidery are good quality royal icing, piping bags and tubes (tips). It is essential to use a fine piping tube. Although time-consuming, a fine tube gives much better results.

Design Ideas

If you need help finding a design to copy, your local library will have a good selection of books on embroidery, and you can use cross stitch or beadwork designs from the many magazines on the market.

If you draw your own designs, use graph paper and colour pencils, each small square representing one cross or bead. Real pieces of hand-made lace can also be used; place the lace beneath a sheet of plastic, cover with non-stick paper (parchment), and either draw and then pipe, or pipe directly over the lines of lace on to the paper. When dry, the whole piece can be transferred to the cake.

Basic Recipes

Royal Icing 1

It is essential that all equipment is scalded with hot water and washing-up liquid (detergent) before use.

5 teaspoons egg white substitute (albumen) powder
155ml (5fl oz/⅔ cup) cold water
750g (1½lb/4½ cups) icing (confectioners') sugar, sifted

1 Whisk the egg white powder and water together and sieve into the bowl of an electric mixer. Add the icing sugar, keeping back 2–3 teaspoons. (It is easier to add more sugar than to make more solution to gain the right consistency.)

2 Using the beater attachment on the mixer, mix on a low speed to incorporate the icing sugar – the mixture should be soft and shiny at this stage. Continue beating on medium speed for 3–5 minutes. (It is impossible to over-beat royal icing as it can be stirred back down to remove any excess air which may have been incorporated.)

3 To test that the icing is ready, draw a palette knife (spatula) through the mixture and lift out a small quantity; this should form a firm peak. If the consistency is too soft, either beat in the remaining icing sugar or continue to beat the mixture for a few more minutes.

4 To store the icing, scrape down the bowl sides so that they are free of icing, and push either a piece of cling film (plastic wrap) or a plastic bag on to the surface of the icing. Cover the bowl with a clean, damp cloth. Alternatively, place the mixture in an airtight container, cover the surface with cling film, and cover with a lid. Do not store in the refrigerator, but keep in a cool place. To revive the icing before use, simply re-beat on medium speed.

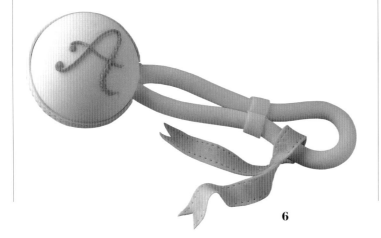

Royal Icing 2

2 large egg whites or 15g (½oz) pure albumen powder with 5 tablespoons water
500g (1lb/3 cups) icing (confectioners') sugar, sifted

1 Put the egg whites in a bowl and, using a wire whisk, rotary whisk or hand-held electric mixer on medium speed, whisk until frothy. Change to the beater attachment (if using an electric mixer), and gradually add the icing sugar until the desired consistency is achieved.

2 The icing is ready when peaks have formed. If the icing is too firm, it can be let down with the addition of a little more egg white. Store as for Royal Icing 1.

Sugar Glue

This standard recipe is used extensively for sticking paste to paste and is not only edible, but palatable too.

155ml (5fl oz/ ⅔ cup) cold water
30g (1oz) sugarpaste (rolled fondant), broken into pieces
3 teaspoons clear alcohol (vodka or white rum)

1 Place the water and sugarpaste pieces in a small bowl and heat in a microwave for about 30 seconds, until softened. Sieve into another bowl and stir in the vodka or rum.

2 Alternatively, add 155ml (5fl oz/ ⅔ cup) boiling water to the sugarpaste pieces in a heatproof bowl and stir. Place over a saucepan of boiling water and continue stirring until all the sugarpaste pieces have melted. Sieve as above, then add the vodka or rum.

3 Transfer the glue to a jar, seal and store in a cool place or in the bottom of the refrigerator.

Gum Glue

This adhesive is used for gluing together separate petals and other elements of off-set pieces before attaching to a cake. (Note that dry off-set items are always attached to the cake with royal icing and not gum glue.)

3 teaspoons tepid water
½ teaspoon CMC (gum tragacanth substitute) or gum tragacanth

1 Put the water in a small bowl, and sprinkle in the CMC or gum tragacanth. Whisk vigorously for a few seconds, until thick. If it is too thick, add a few more drops of water.

2 Gum glue can be stored in a small bottle in the refrigerator for a few weeks.

Mexican Paste

The consistency of this paste should be elastic when first made. It sets and dries hard and is ideal for off-set pieces where strength is required. All the paste creations in this book are made with Mexican Paste or Mexican Paste 2 (see right).

250g (8oz/1½ cups) icing (confectioners') sugar, sifted
3 teaspoons CMC (gum tragacanth substitute) or gum tragacanth
2 teaspoons liquid glucose
6–7 teaspoons cold water

1 Sift the icing sugar and CMC or gum tragacanth together on to a work surface, and form a well in the centre. Add the liquid glucose and 6 teaspoons water, and mix all the ingredients together. You may need to add the remaining 1 teaspoon water if the paste appears dry, or is crumbly or cracking. Knead until all the ingredients are well blended.

2 To store, divide the paste into three or four portions, double wrap each portion with plastic, expelling all the air, and seal in an airtight container. Store in a cool place for up to 6 weeks.

Mexican Paste 2

For a softer set paste that is more pliable to use, follow the recipe and method for Mexican Paste and incorporate an equal quantity of sugarpaste (rolled fondant) at the end of step 1. This pliable paste is suitable for appliqué work, smocking and small off-set pieces. To store, double wrap in plastic and store in an airtight container in a cool place for up to 3 months.

Satin Sampler Christening Cake

This very pretty cake features a personalized sampler decorated with little figures, and complemented by a coordinating bib and rattle.

Materials

25cm (10 inch) long octagonal cake
Apricot glaze
1.25kg (2½lb) almond paste (marzipan)
1.25kg (2½lb) pale pink sugarpaste (rolled fondant)
Sugar glue
185g (6oz) mexican paste
185g (6oz) white sugarpaste
125g (4oz/ ½cup) royal icing
Selection of paste food colours, including pink
Clear alcohol

Equipment

36cm (14 inch) long octagonal board covered with pink foil or sugarpaste
Quilting tool/stitch wheel
Open weave fabric (at least 25x10cm/10x4 inches)
Rotary cutter or sharp knife
Sponge foam
Tracing paper and pencil
Scriber
Piping bags
Nos. 0 and 1 piping tubes (tips)
Ball mould from bell and ball set

Preparation

1 Brush the cake with apricot glaze and cover with almond paste. Coat with pale pink sugarpaste. Place on the covered board.

2 Trim the base of the cake with 2.5cm (1 inch) wide strips of pale pink sugarpaste, embossed with a quilting tool. Secure with sugar glue.

Sampler

3 Blend the mexican paste with the white sugar-paste, kneading well. Roll out and texture by placing a piece of open weave fabric over the paste before the final rolling. Using a sharp knife or rotary cutter, cut out an oblong measuring 23x7.5cm (9x3 inches), and two triangles to create the supports. Place on a piece of dry sponge foam and leave to dry for at least 24 hours.

4 Using a pencil and a strip of tracing paper the same size as the sampler, carefully trace the letters from the alphabet on pages 46–47 to make up the required name. Place the

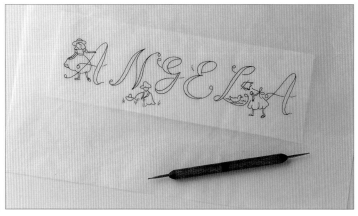

border strips about 1cm (½ inch) wide. Sponge the surface with a blend of pink colour and alcohol before securing with sugar glue to form a frame around the sampler. Indent with the back of a knife before the paste has set.

 8 Attach the triangular supports to the back of the sampler with paste softened with sugar glue, and allow to dry.

paper in position on the sampler and firmly but gently scribe the design on to the paste.

5 Using a no. 1 piping tube and pink royal icing, pipe the wide parts of the lettering using a series of short diagonal lines to create the satin stitch effect. Complete the letters with single piped lines and bulbs.

6 Using royal icing in a variety of colours and a no. 0 piping tube, pipe the outlines of the figures, using a little extra pressure to create the arms, legs, feet and ducks.

7 Roll out some more blended paste, and cut

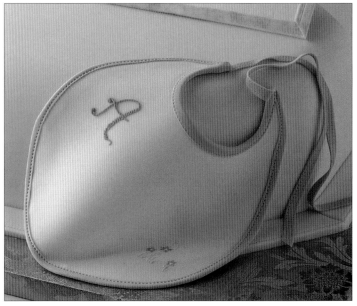

Bib

9 Prepare a paper template and use as a pattern to cut the bib from rolled-out blended paste. Curve, shape and place to dry on sponge foam.

10 Trim the bib with a strip of pink paste glued over the edges, and use the quilting tool to create the stitched effect.

11 Pipe an initial in satin stitch using the same method as for the sampler, and complete with piped flowers.

Rattle

12 Using a ball mould and some blended paste, mould two ball halves. Cut a small semi-circle out of the edge of each half, and allow to dry.

13 Roll a sausage of white paste about 13cm (5 inches) long. Fold in half and gently curve to create the handle.

Wrap a small strip of white paste around the handle to help keep it in shape. Leave to dry.

14 Join the two ball halves together with paste softened with sugar glue, securing the handle into the hole created by the cut-out semi-circles.

15 Cover the join on the ball with a strip of pink paste, and decorate with a piped 'satin stitch' initial. Cut a strip of pink paste, cut a 'V' in each end, decorate the edges with a quilting tool, and thread through the handle of the rattle. Place the rattle on the board at the base of the cake, securing with a little paste softened with sugar glue. Arrange the ribbon decoratively while soft.

16 Secure the framed sampler and bib on the cake.

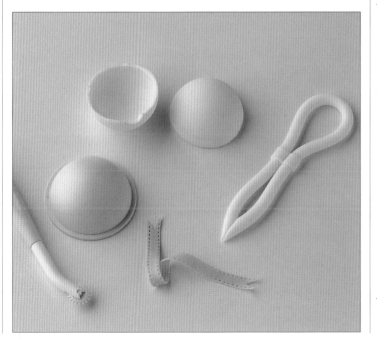

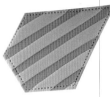

Patchwork Bag

This unusually shaped cake is decorated with colour-coordinated sugar material patchwork.

Materials

20cm (8 inch) bell-shaped madeira cake
Jam and buttercream
500g (1lb) cream sugarpaste (rolled fondant)
185g (6oz) white sugarpaste
185g (6oz) mexican paste
Selection of paste food colours, including cream, pink and green
Sugar glue
Ribbons to trim board

Equipment

Guide sticks
Mini cutters (leaf, heart, etc.)
Herb cutter (optional)
Green food colour pen
Patchwork cutter set
Quilting tool/stitch wheel
Flower embosser
Scalloped cutter
Long octagonal cutter
Clay gun with discs (optional)
25cm (10 inch) oval cake board covered with sugarpaste and crimped

Preparing the cake

1 Cut the cake to form a bag shape. Layer with jam and buttercream, and apply a little cream sugarpaste in places to improve the shape.

2 Coat the entire cake with cream sugarpaste, smooth and allow to dry.

Patchwork patterns

3 Blend the white sugarpaste with the mexican paste, kneading well. Colour batches cream and shades of pink and green. Roll out pink and green paste, using guide sticks to obtain an even thickness. Cover with plastic to prevent drying.

4 Using mini-cutters, create decorative coloured material patterns, and with the herb cutter (or a sharp knife) and food pen make stripe effects. With patchwork cutters, cut out enough patterned and plain diamond shapes to decorate the bag.

First row

5 Cut one point from each of the base diamonds to create the small triangles to fit in between each of the patchwork pieces at the base of the cake.

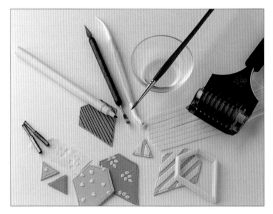

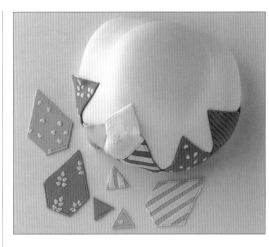

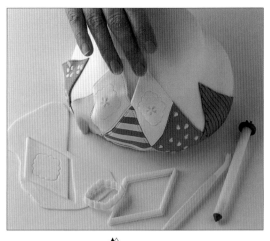

Emboss the edge of each patch with the quilting tool to create stitches. Paint the bag with sugar glue and attach patches starting at the base of the bag.

Second row

6 Roll and cut several cream patchwork pieces. Emboss with a centre flower and scalloped shape, and mark with the quilting tool.

7 Paint the edges of the first row of patches and the cake with glue, and apply the pieces, creating shape and interest by gently gathering.

Third row

8 Repeat the first row, but gathering the paste more towards the top.

Lid

9 Cut a long octagonal shape from cream paste, and secure a pink cut-out diamond in the centre. Mark and

emboss as for the cream diamonds. Edge the pink diamond with a pale green border, and emboss the lid with a diamond design using the quilting tool.

10 Trim the lid and the top of the bag with a strip of dark pink blended paste, cut using the herb cutter (or knife) and secured with sugar glue.

11 Make a tassel using a clay gun fitted with a hair disc, using matching coloured paste. Alternatively, push the paste through a sieve or roll fine strands and make into a tassel. Attach to the front of the bag.

12 Place the cake on the sugarpaste-covered board and trim the edges with ribbons.

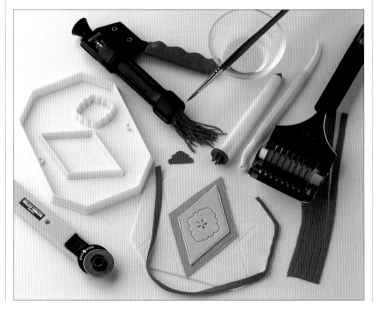

Fuchsia Greetings Card

This design uses appliqué, a simple embroidery technique which involves attaching separate decorations or trimmings to a piece of work. In this case, sugar flowers and leaves are attached to a free-standing card shape. Use as a cake decoration, table centrepiece or dinner-party favour.

Materials

200g (7oz) mexican paste
Lavender, pink and green paste food colours
Gum glue
Fine stamens
Royal icing

Equipment

Arch cutter or template
Window stencil
Soft foam
Small carnation cutter
Small rose calyx or fuchsia cutter
Plain cone tool
Plain leaf cutters
No. 0 writing tube (tip)

Card base

1 Roll out some white mexican paste to 2.5mm (⅛ inch) thick, and cut out a shape, using a large arch cutter or a thin card template. Using a window stencil and a craft knife, cut out the window frame. Colour some mexican paste pale green, roll out to the same thickness, and cut out another arch shape for the back of the card. Place both pieces on soft foam to dry.

Fuchsias

2 Colour 30g (1oz) mexican paste dark lavender. Roll out thinly, and cut out several skirt petal shapes using a small carnation cutter. Frill the edges using a paintbrush handle. Paint a glue line from the edge to the centre of one petal and fold in half. Paint glue on one third, fold over and stick, then turn the piece over and repeat, creating a concertina (accordion) fold. Repeat with the other petals.

3 Pinch the top part of each petal to create a slight point, and push three fine stamens into the centre of the frilled petals.

4 Colour 30g (1oz) paste deep pink. Using the

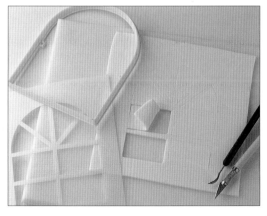

mexican hat method, cut out top petal sections using a small rose calyx or fuchsia cutter. (If using a calyx cutter, remove one of the petals.) Thin the 'arm' petals with a paintbrush handle, and hollow out with a plain cone tool. Push the 'arm' petals back slightly. Place on a flat surface, glue the hollow and push the skirt petal into the top petal section, keeping one side flat. Repeat for the other flowers and leave to dry.

Buds and leaves

5 Roll balls of various sizes from the pink paste, and pinch into a teardrop shape. Mark the tapered end with scissors to resemble unopened petals.

6 From green paste, cut and vein a selection of small leaves.

Assembly

7 Lightly mark a branch and flower stem design on the green card back. This can be done freehand with a food pen or scriber, or using a tracing.

8 Colour a small amount of royal icing green. Using a no. 0 writing tube, pipe the branch and flower stems.

9 Attach the flowers and buds with royal icing, creating a branch of fuchsia. Add the leaves to the top part of the plant.

10 Roll and cut a thin strip of white paste, glue and attach to the card edge. Cut a thicker strip of paste, 7.5 x 2.5cm (3 x 1 inch), and attach to the left-hand side of the card front. (This will allow the card to open without the front section touching the flowers.)

11 Stand the card up and attach the window piece to the thick paste strip with royal icing. Allow to set. Use as a separate decorative piece, or stand on a cake as a free-standing item.

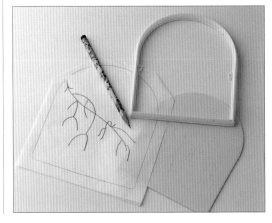

Cross Stitch Building Blocks

These delightful blocks can be used as a christening or first birthday cake. The colours are bold and bright, but softer pastels could be used instead. The children's cross stitch designs can be changed as required.

Materials

1kg (2lb) white sugarpaste
(rolled fondant)
250g (8oz) mexican paste
200g (7oz/1 cup) royal icing
Primary paste food colours
Three 10cm (4 inch) cubes of
madeira cake
Buttercream
Gum glue

Equipment

Fine ribbed rolling pin
Foam pad
Graph paper
Coloured pencils
Piping bags
3 No. 0 writing tubes (tips)
Herb cutter (optional)
30cm (12 inch) square cake
board covered with red foil

Cross stitch panels

1 Blend 250g (8oz) sugar-paste with the mexican paste, kneading well. Roll out the paste 2.5mm (⅛ inch) thick, and roll a ribbed rolling pin over it. Turn the paste through 90° and re-roll with the ribbed pin to form tiny squares. Cut out twelve 10cm (4 inch) squares and place on foam to dry.

2 Using graph paper, draw six different pictures to fit the cube sides. Colour with pencils, using only a few colours per design. (Use pictures from cross stitch pattern books, or copy the designs on pages 20–21.)

Piping

3 Colour batches of royal icing in a selection of colours for each picture. Put into piping bags fitted with no. 0 writing tubes. Start by finding the centre of the design and the centre square on the cut-out panel. Count the squares to find the top centre. Pipe tiny crosses in each square, starting from the top left of the design and work-ing in a horizontal line. Count the rows, filling in with crosses and making sure that all the stitches are started in the same way. Change colours as required in each row. (Try not to change direction when piping.)

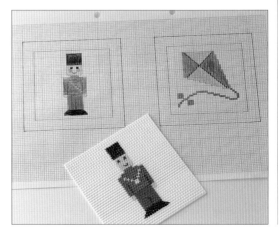

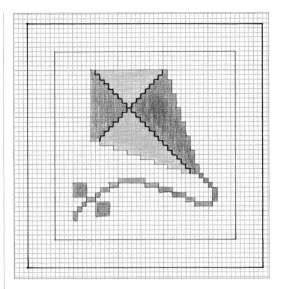

4 Allow to dry for 24 hours. Any facial features or additional straight lines are piped when the main cross stitches have dried.

Assembly

5 Coat the sides of the cake cubes with a thin layer of buttercream. Roll out the remaining sugarpaste and cover five sides of two cubes and six sides of one cube. Cover each side separately, trimming to fit. Allow to dry.

6 Colour 60g (2oz) blended paste blue, 60g (2oz) red and 60g (2oz) yellow. Roll out and cover the top square of each cube with a different colour. With a small amount of royal icing, fix a cross stitch panel to four sides of each cube, making sure that the edges are level.

7 Roll out a strip of blue paste and cut with a herb cutter or knife into strips 5mm (¼ inch) wide. Stick strips of blue paste to the edges of the red-topped block with gum glue, covering the joins at the corners.

Repeat for the remaining cubes, using the yellow and red pastes.

8 Place two blocks side by side on the board with the third block on top, positioning it at a slight angle.

Belgian-Style Lace Cake

Inspired by a lace doily, the decoration on this cake creates the effect of a section of delicate Belgian lace thrown over the top of the cake. The techniques used enable you to copy most types of lace directly on to your cake.

Materials

20cm (8 inch) oval fruit cake
Apricot glaze
750g (1½lb) almond paste
(marzipan)
Vodka
875g (1¾lb) white sugarpaste
(rolled fondant)
Pastel green petal dust (blossom
tint)
125g (4oz) mexican paste
125g (4oz/ ½ cup) royal icing
Gum glue
Sugar flower arrangement

Equipment

Large soft paintbrush
Hollow oval cutter
Heart scroll cutter
Soft foam
Piping bags
No. 0 piping tube (tip)
Quilting tool/stitch wheel
28cm (11 inch) oval board cov-
ered with cranberry coloured
foil
Border lace cutter

Preparation

1 Brush the cake with apricot glaze, cover with almond paste and leave for 2–3 days.

2 Brush the cake with vodka and coat with sugarpaste, using 750g (1½lb) paste. Leave for 2 days to firm up.

3 Using a large, soft paint-brush, apply pastel green petal dust to the cake's surface, masking off a central area that you do not want coloured with greaseproof (waxed) paper.

Cut lace sections

4 Blend the remaining sugarpaste with the mexi-can paste, kneading well. Roll out thinly and cut out loop sections using hollow oval and heart scroll cutters. Using a craft knife, cut out any additional strips of paste required to complete the lace design. Place all the pieces on soft foam and leave to dry slightly.

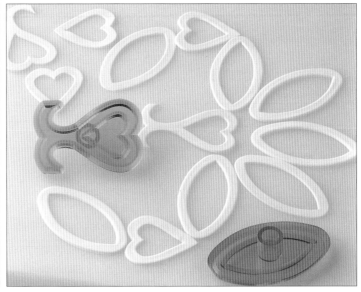

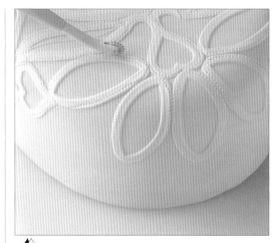

5 Apply the cut lace sections to the cake, building up the design on the cake's surface. Attach by piping a small amount of royal icing beneath each cut section, slightly lifting the paste areas. Additional paste strips need to be placed to join the main sections of the pattern and to create the centre edge. Pattern the outer edges of the pieces with a quilting tool.

Piping

6 Using a no. 0 piping tube, pipe fine joining lines between the lace pieces. Make sure the piped lines join to the edges of the cut lace sections. Place the cake on the foil-covered board.

Finishing

7 A mexican paste border is added; cut out using the lace border cutter, and attach with a little gum glue. Finish with a sugar flower arrangement, if liked.

Quilted Cushion Cake

This all-white cake combines a traditional diamond quilting design with a broderie anglaise border to create a simple but effective finish, ideal for a wedding anniversary.

Materials

25cm (10 inch) square cake
Apricot glaze
1kg (2lb) almond paste (marzipan)
1.4kg (2¾ lb) white sugarpaste (rolled fondant)
Sugar glue
Vodka or cool boiled water
125g (4oz) mexican paste

Equipment

Diamond cutters
Quilting tool/stitch wheel
36cm (14 inch) square cake board coated with white sugarpaste and embossed
Lace cutter
Square eyelet cutter
Broderie anglaise cutter (straight-pointed)
Herb cutter (optional)

Preparation

1 Carefully cut the cake to shape by trimming the top edges. Brush with apricot glaze and cover with almond paste.

2 Roll out sugarpaste to about 5mm (¼ inch) thick and cut out 48 diamond shapes. Attach to the almond paste with sugar glue, creating an eight-piece design in the centre and using five diamonds on each top corner and side. Leave for a few hours to allow the glue and paste to set.

Covering

3 Moisten the cushion with vodka or cool boiled water, and coat the cake with sugarpaste, gently easing it between the diamond shapes with your fingers and using a small piece of sugarpaste as a smoother.

4 Before the coating has set, carefully outline the diamond shapes with a quilting tool, and decorate each diamond with an additional three-line fan shape.

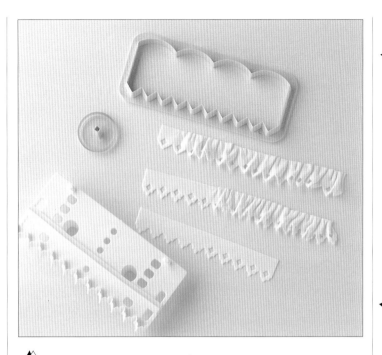

Edging

6 Blend together 125g (4oz) sugarpaste with the mexican paste, kneading well. Roll out finely, and use a lace cutter to cut out long strips about 4cm (1½ inches) wide. Using a square eyelet cutter positioned diagonally, cut out one shape at every lace point. Carefully gather the paste along the straight edge, and attach to the base of the cushion with sugar glue. Repeat for a second layer, using a straight-pointed broderie anglaise cutter instead of the lace cutter.

7 Trim the frills with a paste ribbon cut with a herb cutter (or knife) and embossed with the quilting tool. Decorate each corner with three loops and a tail.

5 Secure a small ball of paste in the middle of the cushion to create the centre button, and place on the board.

Smocked Christmas Stocking

This modelled Christmas stocking has a mini smocked band and is filled with toys, making it a great centrepiece for any festive table or a top ornament for a simply finished Christmas cake.

Materials

375g (12oz) red sugarpaste
(rolled fondant)
250g (8oz) mexican paste
250g (8oz) white sugarpaste
Selection of paste food colours
Gum glue
125g (4oz/ ½ cup) royal icing

Equipment

Ball tool
Fine ribbed rolling pin
Ruler
Flat ended tweezers or sprung hair clip
Piping bags
3 No. 0 piping tubes (tips)

Stocking

1 Knead together the red sugarpaste and 60g (2oz) mexican paste. Roll into a rough

sausage shape, taper at one end and hollow out the other. Lift up the hollow end and create a heavy crease in the 'ankle'. Push the end of a ball tool into the hollow, and press against the sides to thin the paste. Allow to dry for several days.

Toys

2 Blend 250g (8oz) white sugarpaste with the remaining mexican paste. Set aside 60g (2oz) for the smocking band, and make a selection of different-coloured batches with the remainder.

3 Mould and cut a selection of small toys, such as a boat, teddy bear, bat and ball, doll, kite, rocking horse, etc.

Smocking band

4 Roll out the reserved 60g (2oz) white mixed paste

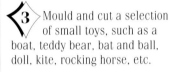

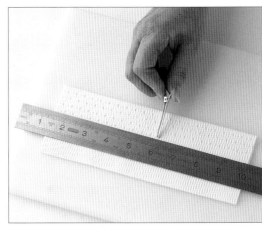

into a strip, slightly longer than the circumference of the top of the stocking and just over 7.5cm (3 inches) wide. Roll over with a ribbed rolling pin in one length, making sure that the lines are vertical. Trim the strip to fit the stocking, 7.5cm (3 inches) wide.

⟨5⟩ While the paste is still soft, start to 'pinch' in the design. Use a pair of fine, flat-ended tweezers or a sprung hair clip to carefully nip every second pair of ribs of paste together in one line to form the base of the smocking stitches. Repeat along the ribbed lines, pinching the alternate ribbed lines, so that you form a continuous dia-mond-shaped pattern covering two-thirds of the strip.

⟨6⟩ Paint the lip and 2.5cm (1 inch) of the stocking

top with gum glue. Gently turn the ribbed band over and fold back the unpinched section. Start to attach the band by plac-ing and sticking the edge of the folded-over piece to the lip of the stocking top, pressing gently to stick. Glue the ends together to create a seam. Allow to dry for 24 hours.

⟨7⟩ Divide the royal icing into three, and colour one batch green and another red. Fill three piping bags fitted with no. 0 tubes with the different-

coloured royal icing. Using the green icing, follow the diamond pattern, and pipe a curved 'S'-shaped line from the nipped paste on one row to the nipped paste on the next row. Return to the first row and pipe down the band again. This will create a bracket effect. Repeat all around the band.

8 With the red icing, pipe a dot either side of each pinch line, directly on top of the green lines. Using white royal icing, pipe a tiny pulled dot directly on top of each pinch line, in between the red dots.

9 Using the green and white piping bags, pipe alternate pulled dots around the base of the smocking, to finish the band.

Finishing

10 With the white icing, pipe tiny snowflakes directly on to the remaining stocking foot area and complete with mini piped dots.

11 Carefully fill the stocking with toys, fixing them in position with royal icing. Additional shapes and ribbons of paste can be cut and placed into the stocking top to fill any gaps. Use the stocking as a Christmas cake top ornament or festive table decoration.

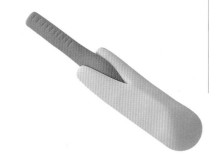

Snowman Beadwork Cake

For beadwork or dot embroidery you can use a cross stitch pattern as a guide. By piping one single dot in each square, the pattern is simply worked by counting, applying additional coloured dots to form the design.

Materials

20cm (8 inch) hexagonal fruit cake
Apricot glaze
1kg (2lb) almond paste (marzipan)
Selection of paste food colours
1kg (2lb) white sugarpaste (rolled fondant)
125g (4oz) mexican paste
Vodka
250g (8oz/1 cup) royal icing

Equipment

Thin card
Fine ribbed rolling pin
Sugarpaste smoother
30cm (12 inch) hexagonal cake board covered with matching sugarpaste
Food colour pens
Piping bags
3 No. 1 piping tubes (tips)
Holly leaf cutters, optional

Preparation

1 Brush the cake top with apricot glaze and cover with almond paste. Repeat for the sides of the cake. Place on a clean board and leave for 2–3 days for the paste to firm up.

2 Mix a small amount of blue food colour into the sugarpaste and blend with the mexican paste, kneading thoroughly. Make thin card templates of the top and sides of the cake.

3 Roll out the sugarpaste mix to 2.5mm (⅛ inch)

thick. Roll with a fine ribbed rolling pin to create thin lines in one direction. Turn the pin through 90° and repeat, forming little squares. Cut out six side panels and a top hexagon, using the templates as a guide. Brush the cake with vodka and attach the side panels, trimming to fit, and gently using a sugarpaste smoother to achieve a good finish. Add the top hexagon, trimming if necessary. Allow to dry.

Design

4 Place the cake on the paste-covered board. Using the cross stitch pattern

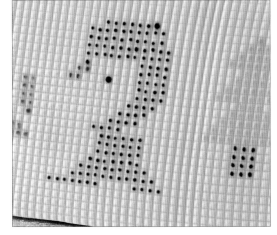

below, mark out the design on the cake sides using food colour pens, counting each mini square as one dot. Use the appropriate colour in each square. Repeat on the top of the cake, making sure the design is central.

⬖5 Fill several piping bags fitted with no. 1 tubes with coloured royal icing, and start to pipe the dot design on to the sides of the cake. Tilt the cake for ease of piping. Make sure the dots are even in size and no larger than each square. Work on each area of colour separately, and continue until the design is complete.

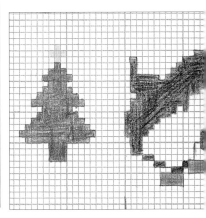

6 Tilt the cake towards you and repeat the piped pattern on the top of the cake. If extra colours are used, remember to use the same size piping tube. Small paste holly leaves and berries can be added to complete the Christmas design.

7 Pipe the border pattern to the top and bottom edges with white royal icing.

Brush-Embroidered Wedding Cake

This beautifully shaded peach cake utilizes a range of equipment to transfer a simple classic design, creating an elegant finish suitable for a wedding or other celebration.

Materials

25cm (10 inch), 20cm (8 inch) and 15cm (6 inch) round cakes
Apricot glaze
3kg (6lb) almond paste (marzipan)
3kg (6lb) white sugarpaste (rolled fondant)
Piping gel
500g (1lb/2 cups) royal icing
Peach, cream, green and brown paste food colours
Sugar glue
3 sprays of sugar flowers
3 metres (10 feet) peach ribbon to trim boards

Equipment

33cm (13 inch), 25cm (10 inch) and 20cm (8 inch) round cake boards
Lily embosser
Ivy leaf cutters (3 sizes)
Primrose cutters (small and medium)
Ivy leaf embosser
Piping bags
7 No. 1.5 piping tubes (tips), optional
Nos. 2, 3 and 4 paintbrushes
Lace border cutter

Preparation

1 Brush the cakes with apricot glaze and cover with almond paste. Coat the cake boards with sugarpaste.

2 Coat the cakes with sugarpaste, and emboss the brush embroidery side design before the paste has set.

Use the lily embosser first, gently rolling only the required part of the cutter on the paste on the side of each cake. Continue the design diagonally, using ivy leaf and primrose cutters, tapering the shape and finishing with the ivy embosser. Increase the number of flowers and leaves according to the size of cake. Place the cakes on the boards.

Brush embroidery

3 Blend a small amount of piping gel into the royal icing so that the icing is softened, but will still hold its shape.

4 Colour batches of the icing in three shades of peach, two shades of pale green, cream and light brown. Place in small piping bags fitted with no. 1.5 piping tubes. (Alternatively, snip the ends of the bags to the appropriate size.)

5 Pipe the base of the lily first, and then the petals at the back, followed by those at the front. Use a little cream icing in the centre of the petal outline, and complete the petal with the palest peach.

6 The brushed technique is achieved by flattening the bristles of a slightly moistened brush, and gently but firmly brushing the icing from the edges towards the base of the petal, following the petal shape and covering it completely in a layer of sugar. The petal should be textured from the brushing, and the sugar should be graduated in thickness. Extra icing may be piped on to the petal edge if required.

7 Pipe and brush embroider the smaller flowers using the other two shades of peach, and the leaves with the two shades of green.

8 Complete the flowers and leaves with piped stamens and veins.

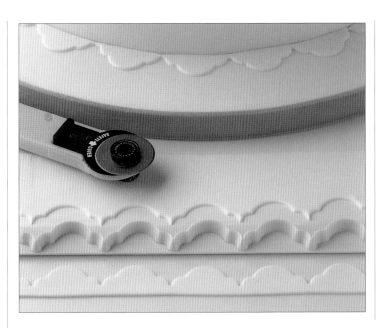

Finishing

9 Trim the base of each cake with a strip of sugarpaste cut with a lace cutter and secured with sugar glue.

10 Decorate each tier with sugar flowers, and trim the boards with ribbon.

The White Swan

Embroidered Badges

Badges are ideal to personalize any cake and can be traditional or made to your own design, combining monograms, numbers, hobbies, humour, logos and special interests. The badges shown here use a variety of 'stitches'.

Materials

Mexican paste 2 (see page 7)
Selection of paste food colours
Royal icing
Sugar glue

Equipment

Open weave material
Badge or shield cutters
Cutters, embossers or scriber
Piping bags
Nos. 0 and 1 piping tubes (tips)

Badge

1 Using coloured paste of your own choice, roll out and texture by placing open weave material over the paste before the final rolling. Cut out a badge.

2 Transfer your chosen design to the badge using a selection of embossers or cutters, or by drawing/tracing and then scribing the design on to the surface.

3 Decorate the badge with royal icing, using piped stitches to highlight the design.

Stitches
(see page 42)

Short and Long Stitch Ideal for covering a complete shape. Working from the centre of the design and using a fine tube, pipe a series of short and long lines. Gradually work to the design edge, changing the length and angle of the lines to cover the area completely.

Blanket Stitch Normally used as a border or to trim appliquéd edges. Pipe a series of small 'L' shapes, starting on the top with a short vertical line, and continuing to pipe along the cut edge.

Couching Creates a strong, definite line or shape. Pipe a line in the shape required, and then, using a finer tube and contrasting colour, pipe short lines at regular intervals across the first one.

Straight (Back) Stitch A combination of short lines joined to create an interesting feature or edge, e.g. pipe a 'Y' shape using three short lines. Repeat the shape so that each 'Y' touches the next at the widest point, creating an edging design.

Herringbone Ideal for trimming edges, especially appliqué. Pipe short diagonal lines, alternating the direction and overlapping slightly at the top and bottom to form small crosses.

Padded Satin Stitch Ideal for covering a solid shape. Using sugarpaste of a similar colour to the stitches, mould a small pad of paste of the required shape, and sugar glue in place. Pipe straight or curved lines to fill the required space completely.

Seed Stitch Used to cover and texture an area in an informal way. Pipe small short lines at random and varying angles.

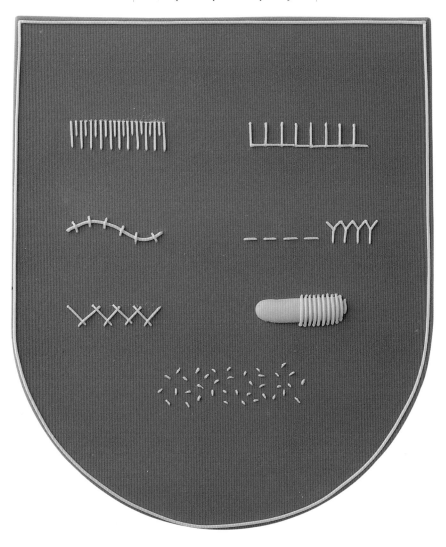

Simple sugar embroidery stitches (clockwise from top left):
Short and long stitch; Blanket stitch; Straight (back) stitch;
Padded satin stitch; Seed stitch; Herringbone; Couching

42

Victorian Lace Fan

A variety of Victorian lace stitches combine to create this beautiful fan, set off by a simply decorated cake in rich Victorian purple.

Materials

20cm (8 inch) fan-shaped cake
Apricot glaze
1kg (2lb) almond paste (marzipan)
1.1kg (2¼lb) sugarpaste (rolled fondant)
Blue and pink paste food colours
250g (8oz) royal icing (made with pure albumen powder/fresh egg white)
Cream paste food colour (glycerine free) for royal icing
White vegetable fat (shortening)
1 metre (1 yard) picot edge sheer ribbon 4cm (1½ inches) wide
1 metre (1 yard) picot edge sheer ribbon to trim board

Equipment

30cm (12 inch) square cake board
Piping bags
Nos. 1, 2 and 00 piping tubes (tips)
Board or flat surface
Cellophane
Masking tape
Curve or tube for drying
Angle-poise lamp

Preparation

1 Brush the cake with apricot glaze and cover with almond paste. Colour the sugarpaste purple with blue and pink colours, and use to coat the cake and board.

Lace

2 Colour the royal icing cream, and put some in a small piping bag fitted with a no. 00 piping tube.

3 Soften some of the icing with water to a thick double cream consistency, and place in two small piping bags, one fitted with a no. 1 tube and the other with a no. 2 tube.

4 Trace the fan pattern on page 47, and place on a flat board. Cover with a piece of cellophane coated with a thin smear of white vegetable fat, and secure in position with masking tape.

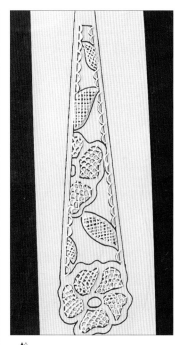

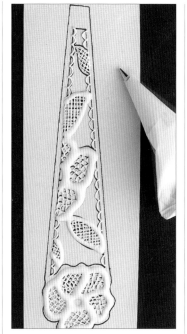

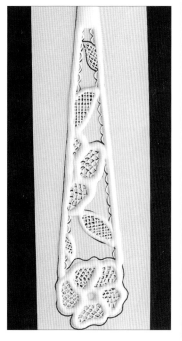

 5 Using the no. 00 piping tube, carefully pipe the scallop, trellis and loop lace.

6 Pipe the straight sides and base of the lace panel with the no. 2 piping tube, and complete the design with the no. 1 tube. Check that all the lace is connected before transferring to a curve or tube to dry. Place under the heat of an angle-poise lamp for about 1 hour, and then leave to dry completely overnight.

7 Repeat the process to make the remaining lace blades. Prepare extra pieces to allow for any breakages.

8 Release the piped fan blades by gently curving and rolling the cellophane backwards.

9 Position and secure to the cake top with a little royal icing. Pipe bulbs using a no. 1 piping tube along the two outside edges and the base of the fan.

10 Decorate the cake sides with a ribbon and bow, and trim the board with matching ribbon.

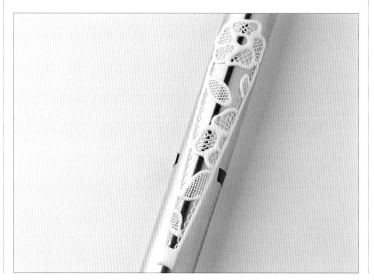

Templates

Satin Sampler
Christening Cake
(page 8)
alphabet

Victorian Lace Fan
(page 43)

Acknowledgements

The authors would like to thank
the following:

In America

Studio 6
(sundries)
1618 Rt. 9,
Clifton Park,
New York, 12065

Sunflower Sugar Art
(silicone moulds, cutters)
P.O. Box 780504,
Maspeth,
New York, 11378

Creative Sugar Art
(edible petal dusts/blossom
tints)
9951 Wentworth Drive,
Westminster,
California, 92683

**Beryl's Cake Decorating
Equipment**
P.O. Box 1584,
North Springfield,
Virginia, 22151

In Europe

Squires Kitchen
Squires House,
3 Waverley Lane,
Farnham,
Surrey GU9 8BB

G.T. Culpitt & Son Ltd
(cake boards)
Place Farm,
Wheathampstead,
Herts. AL4 8SB

P.M.E. Sugarcraft
(equipment)
Brember Road,
South Harrow,
Middx. HA2 8UN

F.M.M.
(cutters)
Unit 5, Kings Park,
Primrose Hill,
Kings Langley,
Herts. WD4 8ST

Offray Ribbons
Fir Tree Place,
Church Road,
Ashford,
Middx. TW15 2PH

Guy Paul & Co Ltd
(cutters)
Unit B4, Foundry Way,
Little End Road,
Eaton Socon,
Cambs. PE19 3JH

Sugar Celebrations
176A Manchester Road,
Swindon,
Wilts. SN1 1TU

Patchwork Cutters
3 Raines Close,
Greasby,
Wirral L49 2QB

Celebration Cake Service
94 High Street,
Chapmanslade,
Westbury,
Wilts. BA13 4AN

Corteil & Barratt
(materials)
40 High Street,
Ewell Village,
Surrey KT17 1RW

J.F. Renshaw Ltd
Crown Street,
Liverpool L8 7RF

Confectionery Supplies
31 Lower Cathedral Road
Cardiff
Wales CF1 8LU

Artgato
5 Avenue Du Docteur Arnold
Netter,
75012, Paris

The publishers would also like to
thank:

Cake Art Ltd
Venture Way,
Crown Estate,
Priorswood,
Taunton, Devon TA2 8DE

**Anniversary House (Cake
Decorations) Ltd**
Unit 5,
Roundways,
Elliott Road,
Bournemouth, Hants. BH11 8JJ